See It Grow
OAK TREE

by Joyce Markovics

Consultant: Karen C. Hall, PhD
Applied Ecologist, Botanical Research Institute of Texas
Fort Worth, Texas

BEARPORT
PUBLISHING

New York, New York

Credits

TOC-TL, © Sunny Forest/Shutterstock; TOC-TR, © cooperr/Shutterstock; TOC-B, © Alex Staroseltsev/Shutterstock; 4–5, © Cheryl E. Davis/Shutterstock; 6, ©orangecrush/Shutterstock; 7, © mama_mia/Shutterstock; 8, © kaczor58/iStock; 9T, © Aleksey Stemmer/Shutterstock; 9B, © ermingut/iStock; 10–11T, © ermingut/iStock; 10–11B, © ermingut/iStock; 12, © redmal/iStock; 13, © Myslitel/Shutterstock; 14, © haveseen/Shutterstock; 15, © Sandrexim/iStock; 16–17, © SaveLightstock/Shutterstock and © DNY59/iStock; 17, © almgren/Shutterstock; 18, © Anna Jurkovska/Shutterstock; 18B, © Martinan/iStock; 19, © Margaret M Stewart/Shutterstock; 20–21, © BMJ/Shutterstock; 22T, © filmfoto/Shutterstock; 22B, © lynnette/Shutterstock; 23 (T to B), © Valentina Razumova/Shutterstock, © YinYang/iStock, © Vitalli Hulai and SunnyForest/Shutterstock, © ermingut/iStock, and © Alexander Dunkel/iStock; 24, © Alex Staroseltsev/Shutterstock.

Publisher: Kenn Goin
Senior Editor: Joyce Tavolacci
Creative Director: Spencer Brinker
Design: Debrah Kaiser
Photo Researcher: Olympia Shannon

Library of Congress Cataloging-in-Publication Data

Markovics, Joyce L., author.
  Oak tree / by Joyce Markovics.
     pages cm. — (See it grow)
  Includes bibliographical references and index.
  ISBN 978-1-62724-844-0 (library binding : alk. paper) — ISBN 1-62724-844-7 (library binding : alk. paper)
  1. Oak—Juvenile literature. I. Title. II. Series: See it grow.
  QK495.F14M37 2016
  583'.77—dc23

2015007548

For more information, write to Bearport Publishing Company, Inc., 45 West 21st Street, Suite 3B, New York, New York 10010. Printed in the United States of America.

10 9 8 7 6 5 4 3 2 1

Contents

Oak Tree

A giant oak tree grows in a park.

It's strong, tall, and leafy.

How did it get that way?

Oak trees can be more than 100 feet (30.5 m) tall.

An oak tree begins as a small acorn.

acorn

An acorn is a kind of seed.

It needs soil, water, and sunlight to grow.

A small, hard cap covers and protects the acorn.

cap

As it grows, the acorn splits.

split
acorn

Tiny **roots** push underground.

A green **shoot** reaches
for the sunlight.

The little oak is
called a seedling.

shoot

roots

In a few weeks, the seedling grows leaves.

Its **stem** gets taller and thicker.

stem

Leaves use sunlight to make food for the tree.

Over time, the oak's soft green stem gets harder.

It turns brown and woody.

The stem is the tree's **trunk**.

trunk

A tough layer called bark covers the trunks of adult trees.

After a few years, the seedling becomes a **sapling**.

The sapling is as tall as a person.

It has many branches and leaves.

A sapling
needs lots of
room to grow.

The sapling grows taller and wider.

After about 20 years, it becomes a big tree.

Most oak trees lose their leaves in fall.

Flowers form on the tree's branches in springtime.

flowers

Many of the flowers turn into acorns.

At first, acorns are green.
Then they turn brown.

In fall, the acorns drop to the ground.

Some of the acorns are eaten by chipmunks and other animals.

Next year, some of the uneaten acorns will grow.

In many years, they will turn into big, strong oaks!

Each year, one oak tree can make thousands of acorns.

Oak Tree Facts

- There are more than 300 different kinds of oak trees.

- Some oaks can live more than 1,000 years.

- Oak trees need a lot of water. Their roots can take in 50 gallons (189 l) of water per day.

- The wood from oak trees is strong and hard. It's used to make furniture.

Glossary

 **roots** (ROOTS) plant parts that take in water and food from the soil

 **sapling** (SAP-ling) a young tree

 **shoot** (SHOOT) a young plant that has just appeared above the soil

 **stem** (STEM) the upright part of a plant that connects the roots to the leaves and flowers

 **trunk** (TRUNGK) the main woody stem of a tree

23

Index

Read More

Dickmann, Nancy. *An Oak Tree's Life (Watch It Grow).* Minneapolis, MN: Heinemann (2011).

Lawrence, Ellen. *Extreme Trees: And How They Got That Way (Plantology).* New York: Bearport (2015).

Learn More Online

To learn more about oak trees, visit
www.bearportpublishing.com/SeeItGrow

About the Author

Joyce Markovics lives in Tarrytown, New York. Her family has a horse that loves to eat acorns.